Jubilee Journal

a workbook
of forgiving
for the millennium
Year 2000 Edition

mary cabrini durkin, osu
sheila durkin dierks

To our sister Frances, who embodies much of the grace of this book

Jubilee Journal: a workbook on forgiving for the millennium
isbn: 0-965-81370-3
WovenWord Press
811 Mapleton Avenue
Boulder, Colorado
80304
Book design copyright © 1998 Vicki McVey
Cover design copyright © 1998 Traci Schalow
1st Printing October 1998
2nd Printing December 1998
3rd Printing March 1999
Second Edition August 1999
5th Printing October 1999

table of contents

And you shall hallow the fiftieth year and you shall proclaim
liberty throughout the land to all its inhabitants.
It shall be a jubilee for you:
you shall return,
everyone of you,
to your property
and everyone of you to your family.
Leviticus 25:10

This is an invitation to plan for a forgiving and forgiven heart in the year 2000. It is in the form of a workbook which will take you by the hand and walk with you the road to a peaceful heart as we welcome the new century.

In our culture, 2000 is both completion of the second millennium since Jesus's birth and also the entry into a new age. Do we wish to continue carrying in this new era the wounds and struggles of our lives, which we have not had the courage or the time or the know-how to heal?

There are those who will say that there is no magic in the turn of the century and the millennium. After all, many people on this earth, our sisters and brothers who are Buddhist or Jewish or Muslim or Hindu, count by different calendars. However, for those of us who live by the calendar which we call year of Our Lord or Common Era, it is momentous.

1

How do we attend to this time? Is there a reason to live for it in a certain fashion, to put on a new heart or a new consciousness for the new century?

The book of Leviticus introduces us to the idea of Jubilee. It is the year of rejoicing, trumpeting forgiveness and reconciliation. Every fiftieth year is to be set apart for Jubilee, a time of ease and forgiveness and celebration. Through Moses, God gave the gift of Jubilee to a people weighted down by harsh lives. It was a time in which slaves would be freed, forfeited lands returned, and debts forgiven. For the ancient Israelites, it was an eagerly awaited year when balance was to be restored. Whatever injustice had been endured would now be set right. Imagine being a slave in ancient Israel, the struggle, the breaking labor, and the knowledge as you stooped in the fields, or made the bricks, or cleaned the home of your master, that soon, soon the ram's horn or *yubel* (hence the word *jubilee*) would sound and you would be freed! Imagine counting down the seven times seven years until the next Jubilee. Imagine the planning for freedom!

What does the slavery mentioned in Leviticus have to do with us? How are we in bondage to our angers and regrets? How are we bent under the weight of our hostilities? What debts of forgiveness do we owe others and do others owe us?

How can this be a time to write, draw, ponder, cry, pray, and dream toward the forgiveness which will free us in our hearts and our relationships?

This book is based on the belief that forgiveness is an intentional process, one which we can choose. Understanding this is an enormous step toward releasing ourselves from the captivity of our anger. When we know that we can choose to forgive, then we know that we have control; we are not victims but agents of our own peace and liberty. Choosing to forgive is a position of strength, not of weakness. It is not to say that the wound has not happened; rather, recognizing it, we still are willing to release the other, and thereby ourselves, from the burden of anger.

Most wounds are inflicted by individuals on one another. Children hurt their parents. Playmates are cruel. Spouses tear at each other. Bosses undermine their employees. Neighbors gossip about each other. Strangers viciously assault the innocent at bus stops and in parking lots.

Our world is also full of more global hurts. Violent racial conflict continues to be played out in the US and in other countries. Gender abuse makes the newspapers daily, and it strikes in both directions. National borders, water rights, the poor versus the rich. Often old scars are reopened when new happenings seem to reaffirm our previous experiences. Fear and cynicism are the poisoned fruits of these struggles.

It is easy to blame others; we learn as very small children to point the finger. Sometimes, however, the person who needs forgiveness is the one we see in the mirror.

A lie told in childhood can haunt us. Perhaps we have verbally or physically assaulted another, or have turned our back on a friend or partner. Perhaps we have been bulimic, or regularly dishonest. It may be that we have told a secret, or taken what was not ours. Even if the act is a generation ago, we may still be burdened by sadness or guilt.

When the injury has come from us, then we need to find a way to ask another for pardon. The woman whom we continually snub, the immigrant group we judge, the child we belittle, the co-worker to whom we have given short shrift, the supplier we have cheated: we may need to seek forgiveness and make restitution.

And then there is God. What do we do when it seems to be God who has hurt us? What can we say when an "act of nature," translated as an "act of God," precipitously snatches a lover's life, or a genetic "mistake" deforms a child, or shortens her life or its quality? When the cry is "Why me, God?" how can we forgive?

This somber laundry list of sadness is built up in years, or comes as swiftly as a phone call or a knock in the night. Such wounds will take the work of weeks and more to forgive.

The blessed news is that this is work we can do. This is a journey we can take, and the destination can be sweet indeed. So, now is the time for increased attention, developed awareness, and even haste.

Now is the opportunity to begin to hallow this Jubilee year, so that in the new millennium we will each be able to blow our own trumpets, and sound our own personal jubilees of liberation.

Forgiveness is, for many people, a part of daily life. When we say the Lord's Prayer, we repeat the phrase, "forgive us our sins, as we forgive those who sin against us." It may be easy for us to let go of the small hurts of others and to forgive ourselves for the minor errors in our lives, even if they are repeated regularly. However, many of us harbor deep resentments, ones which perhaps are a part of our childhood or adolescence. There are memories which, when they surface, can still make our faces burn with embarrassment. There are events which happened decades ago but which are freshly painful when recalled.

There are also the woundings of more recent years: perhaps it is a divorce with great wrenchings of accusations, denials, admissions, name-calling, none of which is soothed by the divorce decree and division of property. The discovery of unfaithfulness in a spouse strikes at our most dear covenant and wounds us at our core. Betrayal by a friend is a stab at all we hold good, leaving us to question our very ability to make good choices. We may endlessly turn the betrayal over in our minds, like picking at a scab.

There are times when the act of another has warped our lives. A rape, a drunk driver, a vicious lie can propel us into pain, both physical and psychic, which daily reminds us of the harm done to us by another.

Perhaps there is an encounter at work in which we felt the fool, or were unjustly passed over for a promotion we had labored for and earned. We are often amazed by the depth of hostility which exists in us when a person who has hurt us is mentioned.

Our suffering may be inflicted by another racial group,

with hurts which are of centuries. It may be the other gender that has done wrong by exclusion or discrimination or ridicule.

Or maybe it is God that we cannot forgive. Perhaps someone has died, or been injured in such a way that only God can be held responsible and we cannot find a way to forgive the one who holds the power of life and death.

Maybe we have been the ones offending. When our habits, our anger, our judgment, our striking out, lead to deep separation and we come to recognize our wrong, then it is ourselves who need to be truly forgiven.

Deep forgiveness is the hard work of facing the old hurts which have rooted themselves in our personalities. It is the work of revisiting troubles, ones which we said are over and disposed of, but which we know lie like small (or large) rocks in the pit of our psyches, waiting for the moment to stone us again. They are even sometimes old friends whom we turn to when we want a reason to justify our anger in a new situation.

Deep forgiveness begins with reaching into oneself, into the core of our being, for that is where injury resides. Deep forgiveness requires a real look at the wounds which have infected us for a long time. Deep forgiveness is a sabbath, a quieting of the heart.

Hold on now, because this is the work of courage.

How do you know when you are ready for this process? Are any of these things true for you?

♦ Your anger has become more of an enemy than a friend.

♦ You realize that though the person or incident or relationship which so hurt you is only a part of your life, you have allowed it to dominate your waking thoughts and/or even your sleep time.

♦ You are still angry, while the offender is getting on with life.

♦ Your anger is affecting relationships which have nothing to do with the injury.

♦ You spend more time looking backwards than forwards.

♦ You are restless, yet desperately want peace.

First you need to list the injuries that will need to be healed on your jubilee journey. In these pages there is a place to name them. There are many lines, a lifetime's worth. Jot down the name of the person or the word which for you signals the incident or relationship. It is not necessary here to expand. You know your injuries intimately - and need only a word as reminder. List the smaller injuries first if you wish. Perhaps you are a person who prefers to approach this process gradually, scouting the territory before making a big commitment to forgiveness. You may not even be brave enough at this time to list the big ones. Have faith in yourself. This is a process. Small forgivenesses can lead to bigger ones.

You have named the work which needs to be done, and by doing so, you have admitted that the injuries happened, no longer brushing aside the hurt with surface disavowals. Damage now can be fully acknowledged. This opens up the fullness of the pain of recognition, if we have not been able to do this in the past. Depending on the depth of wounding, recognizing what has happened and the truth of its impact may open up the deep emotions: FURY, RAGE, IMPOTENCE, SELF-BLAME.

These floodgates need opening. This is the extent of the wounding that has happened.

This acknowledgement means that you can name the one/s who are responsible for this pain. The guilty parties may be unavailable through death or distance. They may not even know the depth of their deeds. They may be so global (such as members of a racial or ethnic group) that you can never confront them all. Don't slide by this step in the process. The offenders may not know what they have done, but you are still wounded. Acknowledgment does not mean that you will ever be recompensed. It means that you name where the injury began.

These steps let us move toward peace which liberates.

Once you have recognized and documented the harm, it is time to take back the power of which you were robbed. You have lost confidence or choice or mobility or goods or self-sufficiency. You will have your own sense of what losses you have incurred through each injury suffered. Deep forgiveness requires that you face the losses. Only then will you know the magnitude of what you are forgiving.

Can you punish the person responsible? The answer is yes. In real time or in journal/art/workbook time. You take back power and control of your own life as you are able to face the inflicter and name the harm, and clarify what you need to restore your own power. This may need to be done in ways other than face to face. See the list of processes for help here.

Name what you need for healing. A letter of apology? Repayment of a debt? An acknowledgement of how severely you were hurt? Listening to the depth of the hurt without interrupting, justifying, or making light of the injury? Part of the restoration of power is the recognition that the injured has the right to partici-pate in the terms of closure, and only s/he can say when closure has been reached. This is true whether it is yourself or another or even God that you need to forgive. In reality, you may never be able to invoke punishment. If you have lost the ability to walk because of a drunk driver, or if you were shamed by a boss who has moved on to another company, the actual debt will never be repaid. Dreams of vengeance will never be fulfilled. Still you can move into the state of forgiving. This happens because it is a choice, a decision, not an emotion.

Deep forgiveness is the utmost tool of liberation, and it is ours to give ourselves. What an amazing discovery!

When the time comes that your burden is lightened through the use of these tools and processes (and others which will become apparent as you walk this journey), you may wish to acknowledge that the act of forgiveness is a gift to yourself.

Perhaps you might make a list of the good things which have happened because of the injury. Did you have to learn to drive a car or balance your own checkbook and so now know yourself to be more self-sufficient? Have you made new friends in a support group? Have you developed greater empathy for others so injured? Perhaps you have found yourself to be braver than you ever imagined.

You can let go of the labels by which you have named your injury. Incest victim, fat boy, gimp. That name which caused shame, and recalled injury, can now be put aside.

As you are able to let go of each injury you may wish to write it on a stone with a marker and throw it into a lake or river, signalling its disappearance from your life. Or on a piece of paper and burn it ritually.

The time will come when, as a fine gift of all your labor, the words of forgiveness will find their place. Such phrases as "I forgive you," "I release you from retribution for your deeds," are very powerful. They are the words of your power. A tremendously powerful image is that you are anointed as a peacemaker. You have the power to bring peace into your world. That is enormous power. No longer the victim, you have reclaimed your agency. You are able to control your life (and sometimes the life of the offender). When you know this, when you exercise this, you are liberated, and you have made jubilee.

The spirit of God is upon me, because God has anointed me, sending me to bring glad tidings to the lowly, to heal the brokenhearted, to proclaim liberty to captives, to announce a year of favor from God and a day of vindication; to give oil of gladness in place of mourning, a glorious mantle instead of a listless spirit.

Isaiah 61: 1-3

B oth forgiveness and liberation usually develop through stages, seldom all at once. The suggestions below will assist you to use material in this workbook. After reading a page, perhaps you will select a process for working with the issues it raises. Of course, these also work apart from the pages of text.

telling your own story

. . . to yourself! One of the first steps is to acknowledge what needs to be forgiven. If we say, "It's nothing," when it's really something, we try to bypass the need for forgiveness--and it never happens. Write or draw the reality of your hurt or injury.

tears

Too often we apologize when tears well up. For somethings they are the appropriate response--a wound not yet healed, an injustice not yet righted, an offense not yet forgiven. If tears come, let them flow.

writing

Writing can be a way of finding out what is inside you. It can also move you forward in the inner and the outer world.
❖ Stream-of-consciousness writing lets thoughts and feelings flow out onto the page, without attention to format, style, or mechanical correctness. ❖ A plan of action has greater clarity when written out. ❖ An imaginary conversation can be more revealing when you can look at the words. ❖ Written resolutions call you to commitment and serve as reminders. ❖ A journal

allows you to see the larger picture developing through daily events and the opportunity to reflect.

artwork

In a material medium such as watercolors, or collage or fiber, you can express and then see what is within, especially its emotional tone. Involving the body helps to integrate the process you are going through, as you work it out onto the page or in the clay.

imagining from a different person's point of view

Can you see a situation as it may have been felt from the perspective of the others involved? Or from the perspective of an objective observer?

imagining alternatives

If events or encounters or relationships had happened differently, how might they have turned out better? Is there anything you can do now to move in the direction of that preferred outcome?

sharing with another

You may profit from the feedback of another person. Maybe you seek a shoulder to cry on. Perhaps you need validation or encouragement, someone to help you take heart. (Beware of using this as a pretext for enlisting someone on your "side.") Maybe an objective person can help you to see a situation better. Depending on the nature and size of the injury, an individual with special skills or training, such as a counselor or spiritual guide, may be the best resource.

communication with a person who has offended you or whom you have offended

Is it time to make contact with this person or group? The answer may be clear to you or may require wise advice about whether or how to accomplish this. If the injury has been physical or if there is a possibility of being revictimized, a mediator or a caring companion may be necessary. If it is the right time, and both you and the other can be expected to be open, choose your words well, either in person or in writing. If direct contact is either unwise or impossible, you may wish to write out or act out the encounter for yourself.

dealing with a person who is dead

The dead seem to be beyond reach, for good or ill. Many people have the custom of praying for or to them. We see this in relationship to saints or to ancestors. If you have something to say to someone deceased, say it. (The word *angel* means messenger.)

fasting

There are times when a cleansing of our whole selves is needed to deal with issues of forgiving. Some find that fasting offers a way to focus mind and body, drawing on spiritual energy.

confession

. . .is good for the soul. If we have truly offended, we seek forgiveness. Confessing to the person whom we have hurt is a wonderful choice. Sometimes, though, it may not be possible, or it may not be wise. Formal forgiveness through the Sacrament of Reconciliation is some churches' way of helping people express sorrow and find peace in knowing that God forgives them.

revisit these exercises

In using this book, you will read a page, do the "work" it suggests to you and turn the page. Come back later - months later- to some of these to see whether you are in the same place. Is forgiveness happening in you?

prayer

You are going to need all the help you can get. If you need to find a name for God which is safe or liberating, now is a good time. Perhaps "Father" is uncomfortable. Try Parent or Spirit of Love or Breath of Forgiveness or Loving Protector. Let your imagination fly. This may be a moment to lay aside previous negative or fearsome names for our Creator. Or this may be the moment to take refuge in the safe, embracing names of old.

celebration

Create for yourself a ritual to celebrate each step of forgiving. It may be as simple as ringing a bell or dancing around the backyard, lighting a candle or praying a psalm of thanksgiving. Each time you feel your heart lighter, your spirit freer, your body relaxing, your relationships healing, congratulate yourself and celebrate. You are making Jubilee!

Y ou are making jubilee! As you begin the tasks which will help to bring it about, equip yourself well. Here are some tools that may help you. We consider the first four essential.

time

Jubilee is a concept related to time, the fullness of time. But we don't have to wait fifty years for it. In fact, if we do not practice its ways for the other forty-nine, we may not be ready when the time comes. Give yourself time for the tasks of forgiving. Select a regular interval to which you commit yourself, preferably at least once a week. These times will eventually gather into fullness for you.

a jubilee place

Where can you most fully focus your attention, body and spirit? Choose a safe place where you can regularly have time and silence. Ask yourself, "Is this a spot where I can cry fully if tears come? Can I hope to be reasonably free of interruption? Can I turn off the phone, or let the answering machine take the message? Can I discipline myself to ignore the doorbell?" The work of liberating forgiveness deserves your whole self. Gather there your other tools, available as needed. If you choose a place outside your home, take your tools with you.

silence

You need it. Especially for deep forgiveness.

your own jubilee symbol

Each step on the forgiveness journey is a piece of jubilee coming into being. Choose a symbol with which to celebrate your progress. Let it be something concrete which speaks to you of joy and liberation; maybe a small bell-or a large one, or a song, instrument or piece of music, a conch shell which brings you the sea. Select or find or make your symbol. Keep it in your jubilee place. Every time you feel yourself liberated by forgiveness, even if it's by just an ounce, use your symbol to signal that ounce of jubilee. Ring your bell, sing your song, play your music, listen to the sea. You are making jubilee.

writing materials

A simple spiral notebook or a high-quality volume may be needed to supplement this workbook-- follow your preference. You will probably want to write or draw in a larger space than this workbook provides. You may need heavier paper, or wish to work with glue and collage, or you may wish to repeat the processes several times. Feel free to follow your impulse as your work develops.

journal

You may wish to keep a journal of your liberation. If you already journal, incorporating this dimension will be natural.

art materials

Loose sheets or a pad of art paper, finger paints, clay, fabric, stones, glue, knitting yarns, hand made paper, paints, pastels, calligraphy pens. If you benefit from working in a visual medium, this can be equally valuable regardless of your skill level.

music

Do you make music? Does listening feed your spirit? Your instrument (including voice) or recorded music can be a tool in this process. Use it, but don't let it take the place of silence.

Bible

Jubilee is rooted in Scripture. If you do not already have a favorite edition of the Bible, look carefully for one that will make God's word most accessible through whatever dimensions are significant for you, e.g., style of translation, type size, literal or gender-inclusive or contemporary language, quantity and readability of notes, or portability.

reading material

There are wonderful works on the process of forgiveness. It is one of the epic and eternal themes of our story-telling. We have included a list of current work on forgiveness. Do your own jubilee and forgiveness search in the library or at your favorite bookseller. Go back to favorites from the past and read them again with new eyes, knowing that they are companions on your own journey of forgiveness and jubilee.

1.

2.

3.

4.

5.

6.

7.

8.

9.

10.

11.

12.

13.

14.

15.

Rituals focus our attention in a specific area: sorrow or rejoicing or thankfulness or the need for growth or transformation. Having elements of past, present, and to come, they may mark events which are occurring or have passed as well as signalling opportunities in the future. Forgiving is so important that it demands a special ritual or set of rituals for this labor.

Rituals invite us into a special space and time. Even if the spot selected for celebration is our own kitchen table, we set it apart when we lay the ritual cloth and light the ritual candle. We know that when we begin we are in time set apart for a significant event.

In order to celebrate a great Jubilee, we may need to plan for and ritualize many small ones. It is by a string of forgivenesses that we move toward the great celebration of liberty. It is the many steps of peace-makings that reinstill our sense of hope and joy.

As we set regular times for working in this book, so should we claim frequent times of celebration. There are reasons for this. Forgiveness must often come from a weary, wary and sometimes cynical heart and mind. As we have practiced ourselves into these mind sets, so we need to work our way out of them. Small acts of forgiveness need to be rejoiced in; they are the way to larger ones.

We need to practice jubilation, to rejoice in the lightening of the burden, just as the slaves in ancient Israel planned for the jubilee year. Their rejoicing did not begin at the dawn of the new year but must have been anticipated in the months before. We must do the same.

ritual suggestions

Small celebrations may be simple private ceremonies which mark both our successes and our continued struggles. This kind of celebration has elements of completion and of work-in-process; putting them into ritual has a wonderful aspect of rejoicing and of hoping for the progress of next week and next month.

Small celebration suggestions:
You might wish to buy a large candle which can be lit many times. It may be the candle which lights your way through the whole process. Select one which is a favorite symbolic color; perhaps green for hope, or blue for peace. A candle with a soothing fragrance may add to your sense of rejoicing.

Incense could be more to your liking. You might choose to light a favorite incense stick at the beginning of each ritual.

The ritual can be conducted anywhere you choose. A favorite rock in a park, your desk, or your living room will suit this process. You may find that a place different from where you do your hard work of forgiveness will be appropriate.

Other possible elements:
- ❖ a cloth or placemat used only for this time
- ❖ a Bible or book of psalms, or favorite book of poetry
- ❖ writing or art materials
- ❖ a new, smaller candle, with the word or name of the offense taped on its base. Select one for every act of forgiveness.
- ❖ joyful music
- ❖ your jubilee instrument

Suggestions for ritual:

Begin with setting the space. Clear the table and set it with the cloth, your instrument, the guiding candle and perhaps a flower. If you are going to use reading material, set it out as well as any tape or CD which will be employed. If you are likely to be disturbed, unplug the phone.

Sit quietly. Breathe deeply and regularly. When you are centered, begin with a prayer as you light the candle. Suggestion: "O Guide to my spirit, you have lighted the way toward a peaceful heart. Thank you."

Suggestions for a reading:

> *"For I acknowledge my offense,*
> *and my sin is before me:*
> *Cleanse me of sin with hyssop, that*
> *I may be purified;*
> *wash me, and I shall be whiter than snow.*
> *Let me hear the sounds of joy and gladness;*
> *the bones you have crushed shall rejoice.*
> *Turn away your face from my sins,*
> *and blot out all my guilt.*
>
> Psalms 51: 5, 9-10

or

> *Free me from guilt, O God, my saving God;*
> *then my tongue shall revel in your justice.*
> *O God, open my lips,*
> *and my mouth shall proclaim your praise.*
>
> Psalms 51: 16-17

or

Only in God is my soul at rest;
from God comes my salvation.
God only is my rock and my salvation,
my stronghold; I shall not be disturbed at all.

Psalms 62: 2-3

The psalms are full of the distress which we may feel as we struggle and the rejoicing which we may enjoy as we succeed. This is a fine time to read them with an eye to forgiveness and liberation.

A meditation:

In this sacred time, give yourself a few minutes to think of what forgiveness you celebrate. Review the injury, the struggle, the hope and the choice to let go of the wound. Perhaps you have not yet been able to fully forgive. Celebrate still! You are moving in the right direction.

Now is the time to light the smaller candle, the one representing the injury on which you are working.

Sound your instrument of liberation: blow that horn, ring that bell. This is the work and play of jubilee.

Prayer suggestion:

"Thank you, God who forgive all, for the good work of this time, for all that has led to this moment. Lead me still in the days to come, lead me toward my own jubilee."

See p. 117 for culminating Great Ritual Suggestions

forgiving another

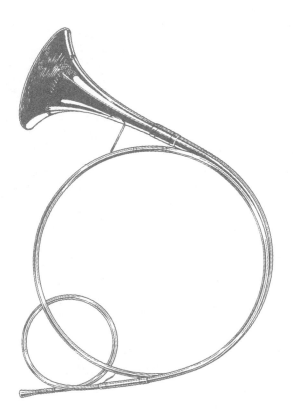

Through the book (later a film), Dead Man Walking, *Sister Helen Prejean, C.S.J., shared the experiences of her ministry on Louisiana's Death Row and with families of homicide victims. She accompanied to the electric chair Patrick Sonnier, convicted of the murder of teens David LeBlanc and Loretta Bourque.*

Lloyd LeBlanc [David's father] has told me that he would have been content with imprisonment for Patrick Sonnier. He went to the execution, he had said, not for revenge, but hoping for an apology. Patrick Sonnier had not disappointed him. Before sitting in the electric chair he had said, "Mr. LeBlanc, I want to ask your forgiveness for what me and Eddie done," and Lloyd LeBlanc had nodded his head, signaling a forgiveness he had already given. He says that when he arrived with sheriff's deputies there in the cane field to identify his son, he had knelt by his boy–"laying down there with his two little eyes sticking out like bullets"–and prayed the Our Father. And when he came to the words: "Forgive us our trespasses as we forgive those who trespass against us," he had not halted or equivocated, and he said, "Whoever did this, I forgive them." But he acknowledges that it's a struggle to overcome the feelings of bitterness and revenge that well up, especially as he remembers David's birthday year by year and loses him all over again: David at twenty, David at twenty-five, David getting married, David standing at the back door with his little ones clustered around his knees, grown-up David, a man like himself, whom he will never know. Forgiveness is never going to be easy. Each day it must be prayed for and struggled for and won.

Helen Prejean, CSJ

starting out

So she wants to see her grandchild, does she? Does she think she can just walk into my life, after all this time, say she's sorry she ruined my childhood, and pick up my baby? I spent my first eighteen years scared, scared all the time. Any moment something could set her off. When I got out, I never wanted to see her again. So what if she says she's gotten help for her anger, that she isn't violent any more? What good is that to me? I still live with all the scars, all the bad memories. I even blow up at the baby. What if I could do something to him that would make him feel someday like he didn't want to see me ever again? God!

❖ *Are you involved? Where?*

❖ *If you're "Ann Landers," what advice do you have to offer to one or more of the people involved?*

First there was all the credit card debt, then I found out about a long-term affair with a co-worker. The next thing I heard was, "I just don't love you anymore."

After ten years together this has destroyed my sense of trust and any faith I had in the values I thought we shared.

It feels impossible, O God
    totally beyond my reach,
    to forgive what has been done to me.
You know my pain,
    You know the hurt I hold.

Edward Hays

Each hurt swallowed
is a stone. Last words
whispered to his daughter
as he placed her fingertips
lightly into the palm
of her groom.

Rita Dove

Are there stones in your stomach?
Can you cough them up?
Must they pass through you?

Read the Return of the Prodigal (Luke 15: 11-32).

Select the way(s) of reading this parable that you find most relevant to your own experience.

Read this story, imagining yourself as the prodigal.

> *What do you wish to say as the ring is put on your finger?*

Read this story, imagining yourself as the parent.

> *What are your own words to this prodigal?*

Read this story, imagining yourself as the elder sibling.

> *Choose a word to describe the feelings of the elder sibling. Is this how you wish to describe yourself? Is this feeling better than joy? What could you do to share in the joy?*

30

Nothing is unforgivable. Many things are inexcusable. Sometimes we confuse them. We think that we can forgive only what we can excuse. For example, untruths told through ignorance can be excused. Untruths told as deliberate lies against us are inexcusable. If we excuse them we violate the dignity of both persons and the meaning of truth. But we can come to forgive.

finding the way

Visualize someone you love in circumstances of great suffering or pain. As you feel the compassion rising in you toward your friend who suffers so greatly, put in the place of your friend a stranger, and generate the same powerful compassion toward her, with a strong wish: "May this person be free of suffering and the causes of suffering." Finally, imagine a person who has hurt you very badly also in these same dire circumstances, and extend this same tenderness and compassion toward him or her.

Christine Longaker

Don't judge, and you won't be judged. Don't condemn, and you won't be condemned. Pardon, and you'll be pardoned. Give, and it will be given to you: a full measure—packed down, shaken together and running over—will be poured into your lap. For the amount you measure out is the amount you'll be given back.

Luke 6: 37, 38

getting there

One of the most public examples of forgiveness in our time occurred in the aftermath of a false accusation of sexual abuse leveled by Steven Cook against Cardinal Joseph Bernardin of Chicago. After four months of worldwide, ugly publicity and a lawsuit, Cook withdrew the accusation. On the threshold of death from pancreatic cancer, Cardinal Bernardin gave an account of the meeting in which the two men were reconciled. Cook had wanted the cardinal to tell the story for both of them.

I felt deeply that this entire episode would not be complete until I followed my shepherd's calling to seek him out. I only prayed that he would receive me. The experience of the false accusation would not be complete until I met and reconciled with Steven. Even though I had never heard from him, I sensed he also wanted to see me....

I explained to him that the only reason for requesting the meeting was to bring closure to the traumatic events of last winter by personally letting him know that I harbored no ill feelings toward him.... Steven replied that he had decided to meet with me so he could apologize for the embarrassment and hurt he had caused.... The words I am using to tell you this story cannot begin to describe the power of God's grace at work that afternoon. It was a manifestation of God's love, forgiveness, and healing that I will never forget.

Joseph Cardinal Bernardin

37

Ask Joseph Bernardin to be with you in spirit, to understand your hurt.

Ask him to help you see a step you can take toward inner peace.

Ask him to help you take that step.

forgiving others

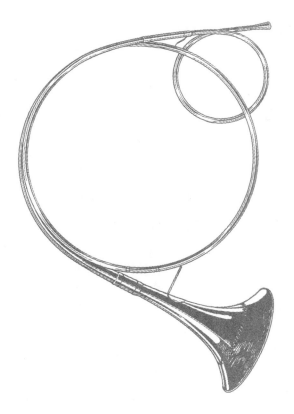

The philosopher Edith Stein, a Jew and a convert to Catholicism, became a Carmelite nun in 1933 in her native Germany.

Taking refuge from Nazism, she moved in 1938 to the Carmel of Echt in Holland, where she was later joined by her sister Rosa. Holland was subsequently invaded by Germany. When the Catholic bishop of Utrecht denounced the persecution of Jews, Catholic Jews were rounded up immediately in retaliation. Edith and Rosa were arrested on August 2, 1942, and transported five days later to Auschwitz, where they died on August 9. The following account comes from a man who was able to visit Edith Stein in the detainment camp before the transport to Auschwitz:

Several times she reminded us to tell Reverend Mother not to worry about her and her sister Rosa.... In the camp, they had heard that either that night or the one following they would be transported back to their native Silesia to work in the mines. Wherever they were headed, they told us, whatever work they were assigned, prayer would remain their first obligation. She hoped she could offer her suffering for the conversion of atheists, for her fellow-Jews, for the Nazi persecutors, and for all who no longer had the love of God in their hearts.

A Jesuit friend, Johannes Hirschmann, recalled Edith Stein's anguish about the terrible crimes:

"Who will turn this enormous guilt into a blessing for both peoples?" Ultimately, the answer she came to was that only the victims of hatred could do it, if instead of letting their wounds produce new hatred, they would be willing to carry the suffering of their fellow victims and their tormentors....Time and again she would insist that hatred must never be given the last word....

Hadn't Jesus, when he prayed for those who hated him, those who crucified and pierced him, turned his wounds into the symbol of love that proved to be stronger in the end?... Hate is not stronger than love.

Waltraud Herbstrith

starting out

It is impossible to conduct a ministry of reconciliation unless people realize a need for reconciliation. That requires speaking the truth in love about what divides and reaching out across that division.

Myles Sheehan, SJ

They have sinned in their greed
And we have let then rob us of our wealth . . .
They have sinned in their envy
And we have let them have more than their share . . .
They have sinned in their hatred
And we have let them make us hate ourselves . . .
They have sinned in their pride
And we have let them tell us what to do (think, feel) . . .

Chris Carol

Sometimes you just gotta laugh!

I never thought of my opponents from a dozen different political races as enemies, but they thought I was one. I was accused of being pro-Communist, antigun, soft on defense, hardline on busing. Sometimes the claims were so weird, I was left with my mouth agape. One opponent said that I was born in Wisconsin and was a tool of the cheese industry. (Nobody in my family had ever been to that state. And just what would the cheese lobby want, anyway?)

Former Representative Pat Schroeder (D-CO)

searching

I was asked about the fears of whites. I knew that people expected me to harbor anger toward whites. But I had none.... "Whites are fellow South Africans," I said, "and we want them to feel safe and to know that we appreciate the contribution that they have made towards the development of this country."
[These words were spoken by] Nelson Mandela at a press conference on February 10, 1990, the afternoon of his release from prison after twenty-seven years of incarceration as a result of his opposition to apartheid.

Nelson Mandela

The good are treated with goodness; the bad are also treated with goodness; this is the goodness of Teh*.

Translation Frank MacHovec

* *Teh* (pronounced *Duh*) can be translated as *Integrity, Virtue, Character, Honor, Reason, Best Conduct, Intelligence,* or *True Wisdom.*

I have been searching for years to try and find a way to forgive the institutional Church for the priestly call to service which I never had the opportunity to have tested.

fifty-five-year old Catholic woman

Do I dare to pray:

"Forgive us our sins, as we forgive those who have sinned against us"?

A highly successful professional, Bernice is active in her parish,
including sitting on the parish council of a predominantly white
congregation. How does she, an African American, do this with a
forgiving heart, when there has been so much sin, white against
Black?

I was born into a Catholic family and went through Catholic
schools, where sometimes I was the only Black person in class. I
was always a spiritual person, but I left the Church for a while,
and I never felt that was a sin. My sister left, and she's never
come back. Participating in the Church allows me to be what I
feel myself to be, a Catholic.

I've forgiven the Church because it is part of society; society
enslaved Black people and so the Church enslaved Black people.
Society is realizing its mistakes and the Church is too. Sometimes
I get frustrated, but if I give up it'll never go forward. So I sit on
the parish council.

Your being born white and my being born Black are not choices
we made, so I shouldn't punish you and you shouldn't punish me.
You have to know how to accept in order to forgive.

. . . Some of us were abandoned, beaten, or abused by one or both of our parents. Our forgiveness in these cases includes releasing the childhood hope our parents will be other than they were.

Maria Harris

getting there

Fire burst into the cold darkness of Coventry, England, on November 14, 1940. A total of 568 people died in this air-strike by the German Luftwaffe, code-named "Operation Moonlight Sonata." Amid the losses of life and homes, Coventry mourned also the destruction of St. Michael's Cathedral, only its tower and spire left standing. On the morning after the bombing, Provost Dick Howard formed the resolve to rebuild, as a sign of faith, hope, and trust in a future which seemed so hopeless in those dark days of World War II.

Architect Basil Spence described his first experience of setting foot in the cathedral ruins. "I was deeply moved. I saw the old cathedral as standing clearly for the Sacrifice, one side of the Christian Faith, and I knew my task was to design a new one which would stand for the Triumph of the Resurrection."

In that faith, the cathedral community has built not only a house of worship but a ministry of international reconciliation which includes relations between people of different classes, cultures and races within Coventry itself.

The Coventry Litany

THE COVENTRY LITANY OF RECONCILIATION

All have sinned and fallen short of the glory of God.

The hatred which divides nation from nation, race from race, class from class,

Father, forgive (response).

The covetous desires of people and nations to possess what is not their own...

The greed which exploits the work of human hands and lays waste the earth...

Our envy of the welfare and happiness of others...

Our indifference to the plight of the imprisoned, the homeless, the refugee...

The lust which dishonors the bodies of men, women, and children...

The pride which leads us to trust in ourselves and not in God, *Father, forgive.*

Be kind to one another, tenderhearted, forgiving one another, as God in Christ forgave you.

The Coventry Litany

59

60

forgiving God

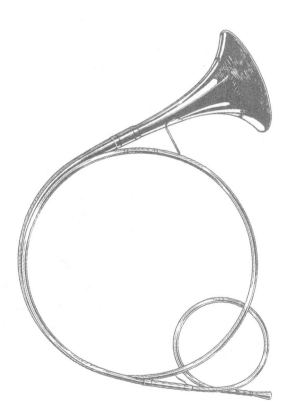

"God, I hate you!"

That prayer, uttered in a strangled voice, broke passionately into the usual pious intercessions of the Mass. It came haltingly from the lips of Bruce Walters. At 44, Bruce has lived with cerebral palsy, blindness in one eye, limited hearing, seizures, and tortured speech for all of those 44 years. When he has a chance to choose his words, he explains that his most basic and frequent call to God is "Why? Why did you make me like this? Why would you make anybody like this?"

In many, many ways, Bruce's life has been defined by his handicaps. "I have a hard time loving myself," he says. "I know people who are more severely handicapped but still love themselves, and I tell them I admire them. But I can't."

When he sees himself through others' eyes, it doesn't help.

To his mother and brothers, he feels, he is "Poor Bruce." "I want them to care for me." When he tries to talk with people, most walk away, though his speech is intelligible, and he is well-spoken, if one takes the time for him to frame and utter his thoughts. "They think I'm no good or retarded."

His anger, which was most acute in his teens, has driven him to trying to harm himself, and to hitting others, provoking some alienation. Working faithfully with a counselor has helped his temper, and he no longer falls into those behaviors. Still, there is a gap. "It hurts to say, 'I'd like some friends.' There are people at church who care about me, but they don't want to do things with me much."

"Why, God? I don't understand."

Job is the scriptural image of undeserved suffering, of questioning, of anger with God. The Book of Job recounts the story of a person whose children have died, whose property has been destroyed, whose health has crumbled.

Know then that God has dealt unfairly with me, and compassed me round with his net.
If I cry out "Injustice!" I am not heard. I cry for help, but there is no redress.
He has barred my way and I cannot pass; he has veiled my path in darkness....

Though I know my complaint is bitter, his hand is heavy upon me in my groanings.
Oh, that today I might find him, that I might come to his judgment seat!
I would set out my cause before him, and fill my mouth with arguments;
I would learn the words with which he would answer, and understand what he would reply to me.... NAB

Job never accepts his friends' conjectures that somehow he deserves to suffer. He listens in vain for an answer to the question "Why?" The author of the Book of Job leaves us, then, with the answer that is no answer. There is no "Why" that can be found in our human categories, to that most human of questions.

64

I am so so very angry with God...

father of a girl killed in an avalanche

66

searching

How long, Adonai? Will you forget me forever?
How long will you hide your face from me?
How long must I wrestle with my anguish,
and wallow in despair all day long?
How long will my enemy win over me?

Look at me! Answer me, Adonai, my God!
Give light to my eyes, lest I sleep the sleep of death,
lest my enemy say, "I have prevailed,"
lest my foes rejoice when I fall.

I trust in your love;
my heart rejoices in the deliverance you bring.
I'll sing to you, Adonai,
for being so good to me.

Psalm 13

I can't forgive God for doing this to us. I just can't. But I know that [at death] God will be there waiting for me.

mother struggling with family tragedy

finding the way

The high percentage of suicides among teens who experience themselves as gay or lesbian is a symptom of a society which tells people that they are unacceptable if they differ from the majority in this sensitive area. Driven to secrecy, many find the dark side of themselves or of others–not only sexual exploration but destructive behaviors and relationships. Even if they have not acted on their sexual orientation, voices around them say in myriad ways, "You're bad, you're twisted, you're the wrong kind of person." Some become convinced that they are not made in the image and likeness of God, or that God cannot love them. Others survive emotionally by rejecting the voices, including what has been mistakenly presented to them as the voice of God condemning who they are.

* Have you felt that God despises you?
* Have you decided that such a God is not worth knowing?
* Are you angry with God for creating you as you are?
* Have you accepted "the voices" as though they spoke for God?
* Are you willing to listen anew for God's voice inside yourself and in other gay persons?
* Are you willing to listen anew to people–gay or straight–who affirm God's work in you?
* Can you hope to thank God for the person you are?

Try praying Psalm 3 from this perspective; understand the "wicked foes" as the voices (not the people) that you hear.

A young couple, after a normal pregnancy, had a child born with devastating physical problems. He was blind and had abnormalities of hip, brain, ears, and stomach. The young father says:

One of the things you learn quickly is not to compare your child to others. Our neighbor's baby is as heavy as Alan, yet he is only a third of Alan's age. He has no trouble downing a bottle in fifteen minutes. For us, every half-ounce is a major victory. Why? There is nothing to say. Either God hates us, or this is just how Alan is meant to be. We may never know why, but if we are resentful, we will kill any joys we might have had.

Jonathan Rhoads

74

getting there

Sometimes we come to realize that in the misery we suffer God is not the villian. Patricia Raybon began to separate the one from the other, and again found God to be an ally in her pain.

. . . God never promised me life without sorrow. Racial pain may be the lot of dark people, but God doesn't have to explain it. I just have to trust the Lord to direct me through it. I realize, finally, that God never expected me to be perfect. Man did. And woman. And white folks. And black folks. The world did. But all the while, the Lord was saying, "Child, you're OK with me. Being perfect is My business. Being is yours." . . . so I will pray and I will try. And God's gonna love me anyhow. *God loves me. And God will help me.*

Patricia Raybon

forgiving yourself

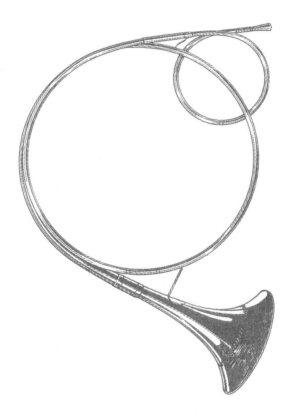

My alcoholic problem began long before I drank. My personality, from the time I can remember anything, was the perfect set-up for an alcoholic career. I was always at odds with the entire world...I tried to compensate with impossible dreams and ambitions, which were simply early forms of escape. Even when I was old enough to know better, I dreamed about being as beautiful as Venus, as pure as the Madonna and as brilliant as the President of the United States is supposed to be.... Naturally, I succeeded in nothing. Until I reached A.A. my life was a shambles; I was a mess, and I made everybody near and dear to me miserable....

My child was being exposed to all this. She was also the victim of my scolding and incessant nagging. I was really scolding my mortal enemy, the inner me. My poor child could not know this. Her father, quite rightly, wanted to put her in a school. When I protested, his lawyer, my lawyer, and my third and last analyst had a conference. She was duly sent to a school, away from me....

I had to go through extreme alcoholism to find my answer.... A.A. taught me how not to drink. And also, on the twenty-four hour plan, it taught me how to live. ... Every day, I feel a little bit more useful, more happy and more free. Life, including some ups and downs, is a lot of fun. I am a part of A.A., which is a way of life. If I had not become an active alcoholic and joined A.A., I might never have found my own identity or become a part of anything. In ending my story I like to think about this.

Anonymous

There are some things for which you should NOT forgive yourself–simply because they do not require forgiveness. You may be carrying a feeling of guilt for things for which you bear no responsibility. If you have been carrying false guilt or shame, your need is to recover from that. Please seek whatever help will foster healing–not of wrongdoing but of wrongly assigning yourself blame.

❖ Help me, God, to know what is my fault and ask forgiveness; to know what is not mine and let it go.

King David desired Bathsheba, wife of Uriah, one of his army officers. Having impregnated her, he sought to delude Uriah, then arranged for his death. The prophet Nathan rebuked the king, beginning:

"Judge this case for me! In a certain town there were two men, one rich, the other poor. The rich man had flocks and herds in great numbers. But the poor man had nothing at all except one little ewe lamb that he had bought. He nourished her, and she grew up with him and his children. She shared the little food he had and drank from his cup and slept in his bosom. She was like a daughter to him. Now, the rich man received a visitor, but he would not take from his own flocks and herds to prepare a meal for the wayfarer who had come to him. Instead he took the poor man's ewe lamb and made a meal of it for his visitor."David grew very angry with that man and said to Nathan: "As the LORD lives, the man who has done this merits death! He shall restore the ewe lamb fourfold because he has done this and has had no pity."

Then Nathan said to David: "You are the man! . . ."

Then David said to Nathan:"I have sinned against the LORD."

2 Samuel 12:1-7, 13 NAB

searching

For some reason it was harder for me to forgive myself than it was to forgive others. I was always stricter with myself. I expected more and better from me. It was easier to justify other people's apparent mistakes. In my mind it was okay for others to be human, but not me. I seemed to have such high expectations for myself and felt I must be the best and do the best always. It was so easy to criticize myself and my actions. I have learned and now practice self-forgiveness. I cannot forgive others properly if I cannot forgive me. When I forgive myself I find the courage to begin again. I now know I do not have to be perfect. What a relief!

Anonymous

86

Alan Paton tells the story of Lester, a young white South African in the African Resistance Movement against apartheid. Under torture, Lester gave evidence which led to the imprisonment of his friends.

Many of us wonder how we ourselves would have stood up to that confinement, those lights, those eyes, those questions. Many of us would wish that even if Eldred, James, and Howard and Desmond cannot yet be freed, that Lester would eventually be freed from the unforgiving past.

After Lester left South Africa he wrote to me:

"Nothing I can say or do, now or in the future, can ever reduce the immorality of my decision–in spite of whatever reasons I had, which I have to live with and come to terms with....I judge myself–and judge harshly."

He has no religion, but I could not write to him in other than religious terms, because what I had to write to him about was nothing less than the forgiveness of sins.... Who forgives sins except God and the person I sin against? There is only one other person who can forgive me, and that is I myself. But to forgive myself when I know no God, and when I am separated from those I sinned against by prison walls and thousands of miles of ocean, is surely impossible. Therefore I took it upon myself to say that those whom Lester had sinned against had now forgiven him, and that I did not know of anyone of us who had not forgiven him. Therefore he must forgive himself.

The important thing to learn about sin is not that nothing can reduce the sinfulness of past sins. What is important is that they can be forgiven, and that, once they are forgiven, one must at all costs forgive oneself.

Alan Paton

finding the way

Abba, forgive them, for they know not what they do!
Luke 23: 34

These are words of Jesus in his last hour. This time they apply to me.

If I knew that my last hour were upon me, what baggage would I like to set down? What heaviness of heart would I wish to let go of, so that my spirit might rise? Might I be relieved to put down that heavy weight now, if only I knew how to pry loose my fingers?

Jesus let go of the need to blame, to have pain befall those who had hurt him.

Finally, he could say,
Abba, into your hands I entrust my spirit.
Luke 23: 46

90

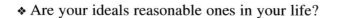

❖ Are your ideals reasonable ones in your life?

❖ Whatever it is that has made you stumble, is there any fruit from this which would not have been yours otherwise?

❖ Give thanks for the fruit as you give thanks for gradual deliverance from your fault.

getting there

Finally, I can say, as Jesus did, *Into your hands I entrust my spirit.*

God showed me a path to greater faith,
A winding, lonely, tear-filled path,
And I stood amazed when I realized
It was the path that I was on!
God stayed with me while I wept.

Georgina Freed

seeking forgiveness

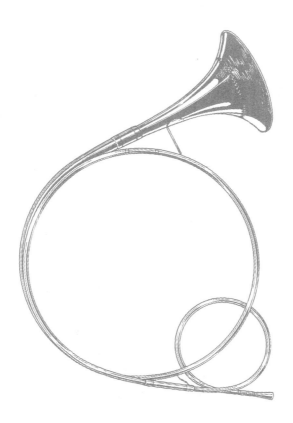

Tomás is a 27-year-old man, the son of Mexican-American parents. He is the first of his family to go to college; he is finishing a Masters degree in organic chemistry at a major western university.

When he was 20 he impregnated his 17-year-old girlfriend, and panicked. He saw that a child, and responsibility for it, would cut short his schooling, and the dreams he and his parents had for his future.

He pressured the young woman to have an abortion, getting the money himself and making the appointment. He went with her, since she was shaky about going through with the procedure. Following the abortion, Tom and the young woman could barely look at each other. Within a month they were no longer seeing each other.

Three years later Tom heard that she had married and moved with her new husband to San Diego, where he was assigned to a Navy post.

Tom has not been able to forget about the abortion. As the last seven years have passed, his sense of guilt has grown. His family has a reverence for life, as a gift of God, which was betrayed by his act. Of course, he has told no one.

His youngest sister married last year, already three months pregnant, and seeing her with her new husband has intensified his feelings of loss, and of possibilities which would never be.

Tom tells himself that they could have worked it out. He wonders if the child was a boy or a girl, and when he sees children about that age he thinks of the child who will never be. He knows that it is, in large part, because of his own self-concern and his own fear that a pregnancy was ended.

Pardon is your name,
> Forgiveness your eternal title,
> by "Mercy as vast as the universe" are you known.

Grant me, O Gracious One,
> your great gift of pardon.

I have searched for it
> in every pocket and hiding place;
> I cannot find it, your gift of Self....

I know it is here,
> buried beneath my pain,
> somewhere in a back corner of my heart:
> but for now it is lost.

Edward Hays

If you bring your gift to the altar and there remember that your sister or brother has a grudge against you, leave your gift there at the altar. Go to be reconciled...and then come and offer your gift.

Matthew 5:23, 24

Until one is willing to face one's shadow, the dark side of one's life, the unconscious simply does not open up, and the forces of healing are locked within....

The shadow is the dark side of the personality that each person carries, the unwanted or inferior person within us who contradicts our ideal image of ourselves and is as inevitably a part of us as Mr. Hyde was a part of Dr. Jekyll. The shadow must be faced if we are to become whole, and for this reason individuation sometimes seems to be one unpleasant revelation about oneself after another....

[T]he danger of an overly simplistic attitude toward evil: On the one hand, there is the danger from the humanist and rationalist who is inclined to take too sanguine a view of human nature and overlook its deep propensity toward evil. On the other hand, there is the danger from certain religious groups that, while they take evil seriously, insist on projecting it in the form of a devil with a metaphysical status....Then we never come to terms with the fact that we are angel and devil, and that the real struggle with evil begins with our ... wrestling with our own dark side. To do anything less than this is to overidentify with one side or the other. If we identify with the dark side of our nature, we are convinced we are beyond the reach of salvation, or, if our conscience is less sensitive, we act it all out. If we identify with the light side of our nature, we have too positive a view of ourselves, and see God as our ally against an unbelieving world.

John A. Sanford

102

A Song of Ascents
Out of the depths I cry to you, Adonai!
God, hear my voice! Let your ears be attentive to my cries for
mercy!
If you kept track of our sins, Adonai, who could stand before you?
But with you is forgiveness and for this we revere you.

So I wait for you, Adonai—my soul waits, and in your word I place
my trust.
My soul longs for you, Adonai, more than sentinels long for the
dawn, more than sentinels long for the dawn.
Israel, put your hope in Our God, for with Adonai is abundant
love and the fullness of deliverance;
God will deliver Israel from all its failings.

Psalm 130

A woman had been charged with a felony which required a prison sentence if she were to be convicted. The prosecution offered her a reduced plea which would have given her probation. Thinking she could "beat the charge" she went to trial and was convicted.

Can you imagine that exactly 5 years ago, my son begged me on his knees to sign a guilty plea for a misdemeanor. I didn't listen!!!

And I wasn't the only one who suffered. Both of my children did, too. My children go to bed every night, knowing that their mom is in prison. How would I have felt if my mother were in prison?

I can only hope that they can forgive me.

woman incarcerated in a Federal women's prison

finding the way

The flight to God's word of forgiveness, which is most distinctly spoken through the word of Jesus in the Church, is not a matter of panic or of coming apart at the seams or of being insecure about life, but rather of a liberating experience achieved through God.... Christianity is this message: we should allow ourselves to be forgiven. And the Church offers us the means: the sacrament of penance.

Karl Rahner

I believe in . . . the forgiveness of sins. . . .

getting there

In Dante's Divine Comedy, *the poet-pilgrim ascends Mount Purgatory guided by the spirit of Virgil, epic poet of ancient Rome. Dante's forehead has been marked with the letter* P *(7 times), symbolizing his share in sinfulness (in Latin* peccatum). *Throughout his climb, he enters into experiences through which he will be healed.*

As we were climbing up the sacred steps,
      I seemed to feel myself much lighter now
      than I had been before on level ground.

"Master," I said, "tell me, what heavy thing
      has been removed from me? I feel as if
      to keep on climbing would be effortless."

He answered: "When the P's that still remain
      (Though they have almost faded) on your brow
      shall be erased completely like the first,

then will your feet be light with good desire;
      they will no longer feel the heavy road
      but will rejoice as they are urged to climb."

Dante Alighieri

111

The suffering of God, or the "pain of God" as one theologian puts it, comes about through the conflict between anger and love: God's anger at human sinfulness is counteracted by the depth of love that is also an integral aspect of the divine relationship with us. The result is forgiveness. The only way in which we can enter into that divine conflict, that suffering love of God, is to experience it within our own lives. The conflict between anger at injustice and an abiding love of the Church that refuses to be killed by anger; the conflict between a vision of justice and the price to be paid in individual lives—our lives, my life—to bring it about, that is how we enter into the suffering of God.

The forgiveness of God is not of a kind that lets go of ideals, expectations, or demands. The call to justice and mercy; the insistence on right relationship with neighbor and with God, each as correlate of the other; the ideal of a just society—these demands remain active within the forgiveness of God for human sinfulness. It is not "forgive and forget," as if nothing wrong had ever happened, but "forgive and go forward," building on the mistakes of the past and the energy generated by reconciliation to create a new future.

Carolyn Osiek, RSCJ

O Infinite Sea of Mercy,
       make this unworthy servant
       the channel of your gift of pardon,
       that I also may be healed
       as your forgiveness passes through me to others.

Edward Hays

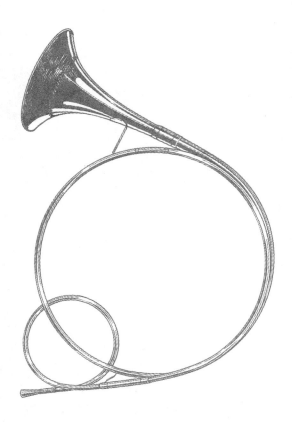

This is to be celebrated as you find yourself ready to embrace the new millennium with a lightened heart. This celebration may not signal the closure on all previous injuries. For many of us that is the work of a lifetime, but it certainly signals the movement into a place of liberation in our lives. When we have put our feet upon the path leading to forgiveness for others and for ourselves, we have chosen to walk toward freedom, and that is a cause for jubilee!

The many celebrations which you have experienced at each way-station on this journey will have led you to know what is important to you and what can be put aside as you plan.

You may want a simple ritual which is a summing up of all previous ones. Perhaps now you will be able to light several or even many candles, marking each act of forgiveness. You may literally light up your living room!

Some celebration elements:
- sparklers
- a cake, with candles and the word *jubilee*
- a gift for yourself
- friends to share the joy, especially if they are ones who shared your pain. If there are two or more who have have all worked on forgiveness, this is a time to share your joy.
- music such as "Ode to Joy"or other loud and joyful music

Gather in a circle, around a table on which your candles are placed on your special cloth, perhaps covered with sparkles for this moment.

Light your guide candle.

Opening prayer:

O Guide to my spirit, you have lit the way on this path of forgiveness and the redeeming of a fettered heart. I have walked together these weeks of discovery, struggle, forgiveness, and hope. Because of you and because of this, transformation has happened. For this I thank you and rejoice.

Here, ring your bell, blow your horn, pound your drum enthusiastically.

Now light one of the smaller candles.

Suggested words:

I rejoice in forgiving _____.

It is joyful to be free of this burden.

Again sound your instrument joyfully.

Repeat this as you light each of the smaller candles.

Suggested prayer:

Loving Peacemaker, you have invited us to forgive seven times seven, even seventy times seven. It is a mighty and difficult task. But you have been with me every day on this road and you have led me to this time of Jubilee. It is a time of liberation. Entering a land full of your harvest, we find it is holy and full of hope.

You have led me out of my own bondage and into a land of jubilee. I see it, and it is good!

118

Again sound the instruments.

Read or pray the *Prayer of St Francis* (printed inside the back cover of this book).

Conclusion:

If there are several present, conclude with a sign of peace. If you are alone, place your hands on your head or shoulders or on your chest in a sign of blessing yourself, your work, your liberated heart.

Blow your horns, light your sparklers, play your music, cut the cake.

Open champagne, toast the new millennium, after all, this is the beginning of *your* new era. Share with each other any plans about how to celebrate your new freedom.

Give gifts, perhaps a piece of jewelry, such as a tiny silver horn on a chain, or on a key ring, as a memento of the jubilee you have earned, and as a reminder to keep on forgiving in the years to come.

Praise God with trumpets, with harps and whistles, drums and
voices, with all manner of joyful noise!
Praise God and the final goodness of the human heart that
forgiveness is possible.

Alighieri, Dante, *The Divine Comedy, Vol. II, Purgatory,* trans Mark Musa, New York: Penguin Books, 1987, Canto XII, vv. 115-126.

Bernardin, Joseph Cardinal, *The Gift of Peace,* Chicago: Loyola Press, 1996, pp. 34-38.

Carol, Chris, "Hallowmass Liturgy" in Rosemary Radford Ruether, *Women-Church,* San Francisco: Harper & Row, 1985, p. 227.

Coventry Cathedral

Estes, Clarissa Pinkola, *Women Who Run With The Wolves,* Ballantine Books, 1992.

Dove, Rita, "Promises" in *Thomas and Beulah* in *Selected Poems,* New York: Vintage Books, a division of Random House, 1993, p. 178.

Freed, Georgina "While I Wept," *Women Psalms*, compiled by Julia Ahlers, Rosemary Broughton, Carl Koch, Winona, MN: Saint Mary's Press, 1992, p. 47.

Harris, Maria, *Jubilee Time: Celebrating Women, Spirit, and the Advent of Age,* New York, Bantam Books, 1995, p. 105.

Hays, Edward, *Prayers For a Planetary Pilgrim*, Leavenworth, KS: Forest of Peace Books, Inc., 1989, p. 175, 176.

Herbstrith, Waltraud, *Edith Stein: a Biography*, translated by Bernard Bonwitz, San Francisco: Harper and Row, 1985, pp. 107, 113.

Longaker, Christine, *Facing Death and Finding Hope: A Guide to the Emotional and Spiritual Care of the Dying,* New York: Doubleday, 1997, p. 94.

Mandela, Nelson Rolihlahla, *Mandela: An Illustrated Autobiography,* Boston: Little, Brown and Company, 1996, p. 181.

Osiek, Carolyn, R.S.C.J., *Beyond Anger: On Being a Feminist in the Church*, New York: Paulist Press, 1986, pp. 76,77.20.

Paton, Alan. *For You Departed.* New York: Charles Scribner's Sons, 1969, pp. 149, 150.

Prejean, Helen, C.S.J. *Dead Man Walking: An Eyewitness Account of the Death Penalty in the United States*, New York: Random House, 1993, pp. 244, 245.

Rahner, Karl, *Meditations on the Sacraments,* New York: The Seabury Press, 1977, p. 59.

Raybon, Patricia, *My First White Friend: Confessions on Race, Love, and Forgiveness*, New York: Penguin Books, 1996, pp. 134, 137.

Rhoads, Jonathan, in *Seventy Times Seven: the Power of Forgiveness,* Johann Christoph Arnold, Farmington, PA, The Plough Publishing House, 1997, p. 119.

Sanford, John A., *Healing and Wholeness*, New York: Paulist Press, 1977, pp. 57, 92, 102.

Schroeder, Patricia, *24 Years of House Work...and the Place Is Still a Mess:My Life in Politics,* Kansas City: Andrews McMeel Publishing, 1998, pp.163-164.

Sheehan, Myles N, S.J., "On Becoming Publicly Pro-Life," *America*, March 21, 1998, p. 13.

_____, *Alcoholics Anonymous,* New York, Alchoholics Anonymous World
Services, Inc., 1976, pp.400-417.
_____, From *The Book of TAO*, trans. Frank J. MacHovec, Mount Vernon, NY: The
Peter Pauper Press, 1962, p. 26.
_____, From *Today* , Emotions Anonymous.

cover notes
1. Raybon, p. 10.
2. Smedes, p. 152.
3. Estes, p.369.

scriptural references

Alken, Martha OP, *The Healing Power of Forgiving*, The Crossroad Publishing Company, 1997.

Barusch Bush, Robert A., and Folger, Joseph P., *The Promise of Mediation,* Jossey Bash, 1994.

Chodron, Pema, *When Things Fall Apart*, Shambala, 1997.

Donnelly, Doris, *Putting Forgiveness into Practice*, Argus, 1982.

Donnelly, Doris, *Spiritual Fitness*, HarperSanFrancisco, 1993.

Estes, Clarissa Pinkola, *Women Who Run With The Wolves*, Ballantine Books, 1992.

Gayton, Richard R., PhD. *The Forgiving Place*, WRS Publishing, 1995.

Flanigan, Beverly MSSW, *Forgiving The Unforgivable*, Collier Books, 1992.

Flanigan, Beverly MSSW, *Forgiving Yourself*, MacMillan, 1996.

Limon, Will, *Beginning Again: Beyond The End of Love*, Hazeldon Press, 1992.

Luebering, Carol, *The Forgiving Family: First Steps to Reconciliation,* St. Anthony Messenger Press, 1994.

Mueller, Joan OSF, *Is Forgiveness Possible?*, The Liturgical Press, 1998.

Mueller, Joan OSF, *Why Can't I Forgive You?*, Thomas More, 1996.